Surviving Queen

by
Slim

Surviving Queen

Copyright © 2021 by *Slim*

All rights reserved. No part of this publication may be reproduced, distributed, or transmitted in any form or by any means, including photocopying, recording, or other electronic or mechanical methods, without the prior written permission of the author, except in the case of brief quotations embodied in critical reviews and certain other non-commercial uses permitted by copyright law.

ISBN
978-1-954932-51-7 (Paperback)
978-1-954932-50-0 (eBook)

Psalms 17:6-9,

I pray to you, O God, because you answer me; so turn to me and listen to my words. Protect me as you would your very eyes; hide me in the shadow of your wings from the attacks of the wicked.

Table of Content

Chapter 1	1
Chapter 2	2
Chapter 3	3
Chapter 4	4
Chapter 5	5
Chapter 6	6
Chapter 7	7
Chapter 8	8
Chapter 9	9
Chapter 10	10
Chapter 11	12
Chapter 12	14
Chapter 13	15
Chapter 14	16
Chapter 15	17
Chapter 16	18
Chapter 17	20
Chapter 18	21

Chapter 1

I felt so ugly about myself" when I was just a little girl. I was caught in a tragic house fire and survived it! Then when I grew up and became a teenager I was molested and survived that. I was such a frightened little girl and as a teenager it was worse than words can't explain but never told anyone but God. I was very angry and happy at the same time, I was good at that. As I started growing and time to go to high school, I was terrified because I knew that the children were going to talk down on me because they didn't like the scars on my face. I felt so ashamed about myself. I had to be audacious because I didn't want anyone to know how bad I felt about my own self. Children can be so cruel and it feels terrible when you are young. I had to keep the pain inside of me because the bullying was everyday. My mother knew something was wrong. I didn't tell her until much later. I couldn't even concentrate on my studies because of the hurting pain the children cause me.

Psalms 7:1-2

O Lord, my God, I come to you for protection; rescue me and save me from all who pursue me, or else like a lion they will carry me off where no one can save me, and there they will tear me to pieces.

The reason for the Bible Quote gets me through stuff. I try to talk to the children and let them know that if they got to know me; that they would like me! But it did not work. It was hard to make good grades because of the criticism they gave me. My teacher was very nice to me. She would let me take my spelling test by myself and that was good for me because I could concentrate. I would cry to myself and say to myself, "(I'm not going to let those children destroy my life)", It made me feel empowered that I felt less about myself and because of that I dropped out of school at the age of 16.

Chapter 2

I was bullied all the time! I finally told my mother what the children were doing to me and that it was too much for me. So my mother said,"Then you can go to a Job Corps for teenagers." I'm thinking, leave home so damn far. I knew that I didn't have no one now! So weeks came and the third week I was on a bus to Cleveland Ohio at the place for teenagers and I stayed there for three months. I got treated there too and I was really scared because the girls and boys were bigger. I felt like a turtle inside a shell, if it was up to me I would have stayed in the shell, that's how I felt anyway. I said to myself "damn, no High school diploma to take back home." I tried to make it work, of course it did not because of the hurtful words coming from my peers. My peers abused me so damn bad, I kept control of my feelings for three months. So I started telling everything to my mother because it was so hateful. My mother told me to come home on the next bus. So the administrator at the Job Corps made an arrangement for me to leave. I felt so relaxed now because I was coming home to my family that didn't talk about me. I felt so shameful I let those children stop me from getting my high school diploma. All I needed was one person to be on my side and the rest will follow. I could've opened up to one of the children and let them know I was also a person with a good heart and feelings. I carried stress for so long I made it. When I got home, I enjoyed being with family for a while and then I started applying for jobs out there. I knew that I couldn't stay there and not do anything. I got a job working as a CNA. It was a job so I took it. I was the younger one there and some people were very cruel except this older woman who was on my side and I felt good now that I had a friend. She and I were friends for a while and she trained me to be the best CNA out there. We worked for years together and she taught me everything. After that I had confidence in myself working as a CNA and I wanted to be as good as my older friend. I was very kind towardstheresidentsandtheylovedmeverymuch. I worked as a CNA for a long time. I started thinking about school and what those children took from me! 'mydignity'.

Chapter 3

I had secrets in my shadow, So I started thinking about another job because I was so young and they took advantage of me and didn't pay me that much. My friend came to me and said girl don't leave! I thought about it and said to myself, hell it can't be as bad as what the children did to me so I stayed. I figured it out I'm just going to work hard and give it to God. I was seventeen by that time and start noticing mens. I liked the fact that they made me feel good about my self and the guy that I met was charming and kind and handsome but I didn't know that he was a casanova. I was with the guy most of the year and I got pregnant by him. That was my secrets in my shadows because I didn't know until i was 4 months and my mother took me to see a doctor and my life went upside down, I knew now that my life was changing slowly and I love it and him. The doctor told my mother that I couldn't carry the baby full term because of my scars, but I did for 9months. When I told him that I was pregnant can you believe he started cheating on me. I felt very hurt and furious at the same time. But I dealt with it and did what I had to do so I called my mother and her boyfriend and they said to me! Don't worry about that he will still take care of his baby. Since I was having a baby I needed to know more about my scars and how it happened because I never knew. So my mother sat me down and told me everything, even the part that her boyfriend was really my father. I had always thought that my brothers and sisters had the same parents.

Chapter 4

I want a better life' OK! Now my son was born and I knew that someone loved me, my burns didn't mean anything to my son because he loved me to the moon and back. I did my best to take care of my son, we played games, went to parks and downtown and this was without the father. By this time I wasn't doing CNA work so I got a job working at a motel down the street from where we lived. But I was still a person of fear with a lot on my mind. At the motel they had me cleaning up rooms, it was ok it was a job, but I didn't really like it but I let them know up front that I could not work a lot of hours because I had a son so they worked with me because my work was good. The older lady that trained me was awesome and I was the best of everything that I did. By this time my babies daddy started coming back to his son's life. All those he still had a girlfriend I was still in love with him. It did hurt but that was okay, because it was about my son. When my son got one year old I started dating again!. My sister and I went to a club and I met a very nice older man. By that time my son's father wanted me back but I was with someone else. The man was so nice and friendly I just could not just leave him and go back to him. I had told him that he can still see his son, so he stop coming as much because he could nothaveme. That ending up hurting me because I knew how my son felt about his daddy. But days turn into months and Thank God my son's father started coming and keeping him son. My son got to spend time with his daddy and I had a nice man as well. A girl couldn't ask for nothing else! All of a sudden he just stopped coming over. I'm saying to myself, 'not again' it was for a whole two month. Then i got a call from my big sister telling me that my son's father had passed away.

Hebrews 21: 1
"Let us lay aside every weight and the sin that so easily in us and run with endurance the race that lies before keeping our eyes on Jesus, the source and perfecter of our Faith."

Chapter 5

Showing Courage Wow, When I got that message it did something to me, because I did love him because he gave me something that I wasn't supposed to have.

> Psalm 86:1-2
> "Listen to her Lord, and answer her, for she is helpless and weak. Save her from death because she is loyal to you, save her for she is your servant and she trust in you. I had to show courage because if I don't then I will fall hard on my face and that's not an option. So I started thinking about school again. I needed to talk to my guy so I could stop working and he paid the way, he was very cool with it and I was staying with my parents at the time. So everything went calm and cool we had fun and it felt like a family and we are happy. When my son turn two year I got pregnant with my second child and he was so happy I guess, we ended up having a baby girl and I had to grow up very fast. I was staying with my mother so I just put in and application where my mother live and that went by your income and since I wasn't working at the Hotel anymore my friend said that he will help if I got it and I did! Now I needed my children in a daycare so I could go back to school and I did just that. Everything worked out for us for a while then I had death in my family and that did something to me again and on top of that my guy friend goes to jail, 'OH my God' is what I was thinking', I felt so disappointed and hurt again."

Chapter 6

I had no way Out" So I came up with a solution that I had to do for me and my children and stop being influence by wicked problem. So I went back to work as a CNA, got the neighbor right next door to watch my children. I was on the job for a while thinking about the death in the family, by this time my guy friend goes to prison and it was getting rough for me. I knew that I was doing to much and it got overwhelming for me. It was all about my children and doing the right thing to take care of us. I started hanging out with my neighbor that watched my children. On my days off I was spending time with my children and then set on the porch with my neighbor. I just needed to have a little fun so I started drinking with her. My mother and father live in the same apartment so all I had to do was take the children over there on my days off from work. I never would leave my children on my parents. When I worked I paid my neighbor to watch them. I also live in a low income apartment so my rent went up and down. I felt so free from tension, and I met another neighbor she was around my age and we would drink all the time until it was hard to get up and take care of my children and work at the same time so I quit working. I caught myself drinking too much because I started getting in trouble with the police, I knew that this wasn't who I was. Keep knocking and the door will be open to you. For anyone who adds and receives and the one who searches will find. Then after I got my self together 4 years later I met another nice man at least I thought he was. By that time I ended up having six children in all and we had fun together. We went to drive-in movies and parks. and the parks. We just had fun like a normal family, but something was still missing from my life! I still felt alone.

Matthew 7
"Asking Him for strength keep asking and it will be given to you. Keep searching and you will find."

Chapter 7

I felt lost in a dark cloud" I went and got same professional help, and we went to Church with my mother. By that time everything change for myself and my children for the good. I knew with God helpI would be better than I was and take better care of my children. But for some reason I still was furious inside! I got some help but it didn't work for me. Every night in my bedroom while the children were asleep I would cry and didn't know why then I realized my guy friend that I had the 4 children with had become increasingly jealous and violent toward me. He got very abusive and people thought he was a good man. He was impressionate toward everyone. He will do things to me that in my mind wasn't right. I thought that if I gave in the relationship that thing would get better since he was the father of my 4 children and also claimed that he loved me. He was good to the children but for some reason didn't like me. But I deal with it because of the children that loved him. I know now what the reason was; it was alcohol and drugs. Some days he would treat me like a queen. On the other hand he was belligerent to me but I made it. Nobody knew what I was going through and I tried to hope and pray that things got better for me and the children, things did get better for a couple of years. He got friendly and playful to us. We went on trips out of town to see his mother every weekend and that was good compassion on his behalf.

> *The people will listen and listen but not understand. They will look and look but not see because their minds are dull and they have stopped up their ears. My children had so much fun and to see them happy was all I wanted.*

Chapter 8

I stayed because of the children') I couldn't understand why come I didn't just take the children and go to my family's home so I fingered if I just do what he want and don't dress pretty then everything would be fine and It work for months but my self-esteem was down and I really didn't care as long as my children was happy! I was a good actor even with my family though so I did so much for my family. I clean, cook and deal with the children and plus with the abusive. But I made it! I used to wonder how my children would turn out and actually they turned out wonderful. But with our God of course we can make it on our own. But I think that my family knew about things, just waiting on me to tell them but I didn't say anything for a long time But I made it. So by that point I was getting very tired of it, so I decided to leave him when I tried to change my life for my children. He tried everything to stop me. I prayed every night for strength from my God and it started working for us.

Chapter 9

I was at my breaking point' I knew that one day my life would change once I got him out of my life, this time I had enough I left everything and took my babies and went to my sister's house we was there for weeks and he kept coming over her home to see the the children as hr call it. He was so charming with me and the children so I went back home because they had to go to school as well so it wasn't really about me my children: we had everything at the home. I didn't want all the drama at my sister house because she had children as well. He was good for a month are two and then he started again my sister made me come back with the babies. Then something happened while everyone was asleep. The door was unlocked and he walked in on the man that I thought loved me. The father of my 4 children was on top of me stabbing me over a dozen times and left me to die but God had more plans for me and my children. My sister heard me screaming and knocked him over the head with a glass smoke tray. I stayed in the hospital for 6 weeks once I got better and was able to go home. He started calling me on the phone multiple times a day. He was trying to drive me crazy and it almost worked.

Luke 17: 5-6
It is by Faith that she understands that the universe was created by God's word so that what can be seen was made out of want seen cannot be seen. The circumstance that was around me made me realize that I had to think about my children. They came first in my life.

Chapter 10

"I searched for safety" I finally got someone to help me and my children. I called the shelter for help. I told them my situation and that was all I needed to get my plan going. My children and I went to stay at the shelter for 3 months and he found us so the manager told me that we were putting other families in danger. I was so afraid and very scared I could have gone to my family but didn't want to put them in harm's way. I had to think about my things at my home and my children. It was so damn much so what I came up with was taking my children and I to another shelter and getting a family member to stay in my home.

Psalm 23: 3-4
He guides me new strength, he guides me in the right paths, as he has promised. Even if I go through the deepest darkness, I will not be afraid, Lord, for you are with me. Can you imagine still in pains from stab wounds and doing everything to protect me and my children. My family was there for me but I feel like I cause the problem so I had to deal with it on my own before I got my family member permission to stay at my home, so I went back to my home because my children school and everything was there and family member have rules different from mine.
And by that time the police had not caught him yet and I felt like I was losing my mind for a minute. He found out that I was back home and started calling me frequently. I was really losing it but God was good to me. The children and I was at home along and he tried to come in the home again so I got my family member to stay with us and he slept in my room because that's where my bruiser was trying to get to me and he did he actually got through the window and he and my family member got into a huge fight police was call but he got away again. I was so….. Nervous that every time someone would walk by me I would jump. I'll call everybody

*to get some help for me and my children because I couldn't
deal with it and still do things for my children.*

*Psalm 70:1-2-5
Save me, O God! Lord, help me now! May those who try
to kill me be defeated and confused, I am weak and poor:
come to me quickly, O God. You are my Savior and my Lord
hurry to my Aid!*

Chapter 11

Became Different' I had to be two different people so my children wouldn't feel so sad for me. You know y'all fatal attraction is no joke to deal with and still do your parental rights as a parent. But I survived them with the Lord's help he had a lot to do with it. God gave me the strongest strength to battle with our own struggle and pain. Don't accept what men do to you, give it to our God until you have been touched by our Survivor you can't be completely. Now I'm a full grown adult that knows that life is like a roller coaster and I have to take it and run with it. Oh: God! All of the calling me and threatening me paid off for me and my children because I received a very important phone call from a woman at the "Victim Assistant". Now this place was far out can't say where because it's a 'hiding place' for abused women. By this time we are still at home with family member and this is the second shelter. I told the woman about the first shelter and that my abuser found out were we where so she did fix it but one thing about that: you can't tell your family member are friends so I got my family member permission to stay in my home until they found him I was so damn afraid to leave I didn't really want to give up everything but I had no choice.

> Psalms 37:4
> *Be patient and wait for the Lord to act: don't be worried about those who prosper or those who succeed in their evil plans. So I did it, my children and I was gone for 6 months and it changed everything for me and the children. You know actually that made my children and myself so damn close and we made it together. The Lord was doing his work on us people at the shelter would ask 'why do you look so mean'! Wow I didn't feel mean I guess it was being a bruise they would also say to me you suffered a lot by that man! Didn't you I would just look at them never would talk to noone one day a movie came on the television and the women were being funny every time I go in the TV room*

they would turn it off. later I found out why they did it because it was similar to my case and once I got a know everybody it was pretty cool there. We had party days for the children and movie nights. I even work there and my children love the school and also we had counselors with your children twice aweek.

Chapter 12

"Face Reality"] What I mean about the sacrifice is that my children and I had to leave a wonderful cozy home to fight satan going to one shelter after another one. because the thing about that man was very sweet: he went out in those streets and came back as satan. Our God place us far away from my abuser where he couldn't found us now days turn into months and I get a call from Indiana I'm thinking what the hell now we may have to leave again but it was very good new they got the sumbitch the children was upstair by this time, so I run up there and told them what was up about the situation and they wanted to stay and so did I. I remind you I still has staples from the stab wounds. That what I mean by 'Face Reality now I have to go back home and see my bruiser because I having seen him in over 6 months.

Philippian 4:13
I have the strength to face all condition by the power that Christ gives me. My children and I were so happy but we had to go back and put him away for good. We was scared and confused on what we had to face.

Chapter 13

"Revenge" Well we was on our way back to Indiana where all the hell was I'm looking at my children face with crying and sadness how done that makes a mother feel but we still had our life in Indiana like my family of course I really didn't want to face that man. I wasn't over the pain that he cause me and my children but I was at ease of what he did. And then they told me that that I had to put my son on the court stand, I was so furious about that he was too little and had to relive that tragic moment they told me that putting him away for 20 with my son help it will work I don't know because with just my testimony if seems like it wasn't enough, because of my son being so little the jury will feel sad. I really don't want to do it but my son look at me and said momma lets do this. Well I pray that God give my son the strength to answer the question. My son did real good: next it was my turn I couldn't even look at him. I was so damn nervous and shaky like I was going to have a seizure. I did it and after that we had to wait in the hallway for 4 hours while the jury makes a decision, I pray to my God while waiting on the verdict. After the 4 hours it was worth it the jury came back with a sentence of 20 years, Oh I was so damn happy to hear that and it was a relief off of my shoulders and I loves it. We was able to go back to our life. In the meantime we enjoying life and having fun with each other and trying to put the past behind us the thing about that the 10 years came very quick I had forgot that back then it was 2 for 1 in prison later in the years I got a call from the prosecute office saying that his ass was getting out my heart dropped.

Luke 1:37

For there is nothing that God cannot do.

Chapter 14

Incredible Life' After he got out of prison the bruiser had nerve to call me well his response was that he wanted to see the children so I hanged up on him the bruiser kept calling back I never did answer the phone after a while he stopped calling weeks go by and that day my older son came over to the home and that day the bruise calls my son say! Momma let him come and see his children. I wasn't afraid because my older son was there so I let him come and see the children. Remind you I had the 4 by him and the girls didn't mind seeing him but the boys: well what do u think! So I figured hell why did he deserve to see the children, I went downtown and got restraining order but I didn't give a damn, I was getting stronger months goes by and I gets a calls from his mother, she was a nice lady to me and the children. The call from the grandmother was that the bruiser had passed! Wow to myself: but I was happy. When she later had the funeral for him the boys didn't want to go and I didn't make them. By the time one of my sister had passed away and that was the one that told me my bruiser wasn't right in her eye and I should had listen, but you live and learn I would tell my children whatever happen it will be up to us but whatever happen God will be with us.

Psalms 37:7
Be patient and wait for the Lord to act: don't be worried about those who prosper or those who succeed in their evilplans.

Chapter 15

I carried to much burden" I deal with so much drama in my life that it cause a lot of stress: but I still try to smile when I was happy and laughs when I was afraid and no one even knew it betrayal is painful when you are in love, this woman ask me one time how do you do it with all you went through! I would say with God's help. I remember my family telling me that I was a strong person and that I shouldn't let a man blind side me. I would still manages to stay very strong because I was a mother and my children needed and I needed me I realize if it weren't for falling I wouldn't made it this far months goes by and my mother passed away in the same year my sister passed. My mother was very sick so I was ready for that one! In spite of everything in my life deaths, stabbed wound and GOd still blessed me. My God saved me many times that's why I'm so strong because God has a plan for me and my children, that man had put a lot of burden on me and didn't care

Psalms 18:48

O Lord, you give me Victory over my enemies and protect me from violent people.

Chapter 16

I believed in God" Even when I was so afraid and didn't trusted no one, I had to believe in someone for my children and that was God. I was still going through a lot but it wasn't bad as before! What I needed to do was get a handle on life because I wa a little lost even those God had me and my children back I needed to started reading the Bible more since my mine is a little better I needed to get in school and Church and fulfill my dreams for my children and be a good mother, I was well like, everyone loves me it's just I didn't really love myself like I should have. I had so much running in my mind and it started coming out. I had 4 goals and one was

1. "Going back to Church"
2. Getting my High school Diploma
3. "Publishing a Book"
4. "Being thebestMother"

My children had gotten older so the older ones can watch the smaller ones and we could save money on a babysitter: so we agreed on that and I went back to work on days and plus went to school on my off days and I was tried too, but I did it for a while. You know they are pitfalls that will come your way, so please watch out for self-pity, self-preoccupation and giving up. My raging storm was over so now: wasn't nobody going to stop me but God! I remember that Grandma used to tell me that! "Who looks outside dreams' and who looks inside awakens! I never understood it but it was about 'what is deep in your heart that only God can bring out. Later down the road I lost my big brother and then a year after that I lost my baby sister and we were very close because we were the 3 youngest children out of 15 children. It almost killed me inside, but God gave me so much power and strength to overcome it for my children. And I remember what my abuser told me one time! That he wasn't finished with me and he was dead, What now! I know what he meant by that because I still have critical pain in my stomach where he stabbed me. I was born blessed because the doctor told my mother (allegedly) that she had 24 hour to get me some blood when I got burnt and according to another doctor (allegedly) I was supposed to die after the stab wounds, But I made it! Another family member said that I was a miracle child. God is my shield and with his strength and through him, I will make it no matter what! I don't know what's out there waiting for my children and myself but God will find it for us. I hope and pray that my book will touch someone's heart.

"Ephesians 3:20"
To him who by means of his power working in us is able to do So much more that we can ever ask for: or even thinkof:

Chapter 17

God was testing me" But I knew now that God was testing my Faith. When you are going through something give it to our Mighty God and he will bring you through it! And another thing don't let no one stand in the way of your dreams. My children are the best thing that ever happened to me and they are the one that made me strong and my God of course. You know God had a plan for my children and myself that's why we went through so much drama.

Sometimes I would think about my abuser and say to myself! "Why did I stay that long and let him Fuck me up like that, was I weak and fearful. Going to school helped me understand the meaning of some things. I was so caught up that I couldn't even listen to music, so I started listening to Yolanda Adams songs and the lyrics and listening to those got me through so much anger that was inside of me. I used to dream of being a singer or a dancing but my God had something else planned for me and my children well my children and myself end up moving in a bigger home and we love it because it was far from where the abuse happen and I ended up finding the school that I always wanted to go, OH my God, IT was God's work. IT was called the "Excel Center" and they was very helpful and took time with you. The school was very inspired and I had this one teacher that encourage me to write my Book, and that where it all began.

Psalms 37:5
Give yourself to the Lord: trust in him, and he will
help you: Like Yolanda Adams said I can"t
think about never giving up!

Chapter 18

"I did it with my God's help" Everytime I think about my life it remind me of "Jennifer Lopez" song (Alive) and I thank God everyday for my life every timeI listen to this song it makes me very good about myself because I'm Alive but the stuff I had to do to get there. I just hope this Book reaches the next generation and to let them know whatever you going through just don't give up by my girl Yolanda Adams God put me through that so I can write a Book and warn people about how bruised can affect your body and mind. When I started writing this Book I knew that it was going to be hurtful for me to redo the past: but God had me to do it encourage me to bring it out on paper. I had no choice but to write this Book, do you know it took me 10 years to get out of a shell but with the help from God I did it! Sometimes it cross my mind and I give it to God that's why I know that this Book will save a life.

1Thessalonians 5:28
The grace of our Lord Jesus Christ be with you. IT's something that I had to do for someone to read it, that's why I put my business out there! Yolanda Adams said (allegedly) in her song go for your dreams and that's what I'm doing, Thank you Miss Adams for your aspiring help. And I'm hoping one day are one year that Mr Perry make my Book a movie are someone, Thank you Mr Perry for your played also because they help me along the way also! My son told me one time, he said wow momma this book sounds like a movie, "I thought to myself it is in some one"s eyes.(Bible Quote) "Ephesians 6: 16 At all times carry Faith as a shield: for with it you will be able to put out all the burning arrows shot by the evil. Amen. Have a blessed and safe day and enjoy my book.

www.ingramcontent.com/pod-product-compliance
Lightning Source LLC
Chambersburg PA
CBHW071424070526
44578CB00003B/685